Hugh Barclay

**Heathen Mythology Corroborative or Illustrative of Holy Scripture**

Hugh Barclay

**Heathen Mythology Corroborative or Illustrative of Holy Scripture**

ISBN/EAN: 9783743394988

Manufactured in Europe, USA, Canada, Australia, Japa

Cover: Foto ©Lupo / pixelio.de

Manufactured and distributed by brebook publishing software (www.brebook.com)

Hugh Barclay

**Heathen Mythology Corroborative or Illustrative of Holy Scripture**

# HEATHEN MYTHOLOGY:

CORROBORATIVE OR ILLUSTRATIVE OF

## HOLY SCRIPTURE.

# HEATHEN MYTHOLOGY

CORROBORATIVE OR ILLUSTRATIVE OF

## HOLY SCRIPTURE.

BY

HUGH BARCLAY, LL.D
LATE SHERIFF SUBSTITUTE AT PERTH.

GLASGOW:
MORISON BROTHERS, 99 BUCHANAN STREET.

1884.

# PREFATORY NOTE.

WHAT is contained in the following pages was written and delivered many years ago in the shape of public lectures. It was afterwards published in separate portions in the *Christian Treasury*, and is now, with some additions, set forth in collected form.

PERTH, 1*st February*, 1884.

The above date was chosen by the lamented author himself some time before his death.

# THE LATE

# SHERIFF BARCLAY, LL.D.

IT may not be amiss to preface this little volume with a few memorial words respecting its highly esteemed author, who died while it was passing through the press.

He was the seventh child and fourth son of Mr. John Barclay, a merchant in Glasgow, and was born in that city on the 18th January, 1799. He was named after his uncle, Hugh Hay, of Paris House, Perthshire—the name being a family one. One of his earliest and most vivid remembrances was that of a visit paid to this relative, and of having been driven to Perth, across the old Bridge of Earn, to see the volunteers of those days at exercise on the North Inch. It was his first glimpse of the city in which the larger portion of his life was spent, and by which he came to be held in such just honour and regard. He received his education at different schools in Glasgow, and was throughout distinguished by his diligence and proficiency. The fondness for work rather than play was already manifested by him. In due course he was enrolled as a student of the University, and attended the Latin, Greek, and Logic classes—taking also a prominent part in the work and discussions of the students' debating society. During the period of his university attendance, and with the view of qualifying himself for the legal profession, he entered the office of an eminent city lawyer, where he continued for five years, learning whatever was to be learned, and winning regard and confidence by his industry, cleverness, and faithfulness. Having then spent a short time in Edinburgh in further professional study and pursuits, he returned to Glasgow in 1821, and, after passing a most creditable examination, was admitted a member of the Faculty of Procurators. Subsequently, and while still studying for the Bar, he became the junior partner of a firm (Russell & Barclay), in which capacity he gave such proof of his remarkable powers and abilities as attracted the notice of those in authority, and brought about his speedy advancement to the bench. In 1826 he married Margaret Buchanan —daughter of Mr. William Buchanan, Merchant —with whom it was given him to spend a long and happy union of fifty-seven years, and by whom he is survived.

The general features of character and disposition — which were more distinctly shown and developed in a more prominent position, and in the enjoyment of enlarged opportunities — were from the first to be seen and recognised in him. He could not confine himself to mere *practice*. While faithful to, he was able to look beyond the demands and details of, his profession. He evinced a lively sympathy with the intellectual movement, which at this period had begun, and was leading to the foundation of Mechanics' Institutes and the like, as well as with that loftier and stronger sense of duty on the part of men one towards another which was being called forth. Eager in the pursuit of knowledge, he attended various courses of lectures, while he took a zealous part in Sabbath School and Mission work—work which was then a new thing, and in which he specially enjoyed the fellowship and co-operation of Mr., now Sir, James Watson, his life-long friend. He was in the habit of reverting with satisfaction to those days of early enthusiasm and disinterested effort, no less than of professional success, and cheerful social intercourse. The memory of them was pleasant to him. He was besides warmly attached to his native city. In his "Rambling Recollections" he has given a most interesting account of its old aspects, streets, and buildings; its old customs and ways. But while he thus recalled its past, he could also rejoice in its present—the multiplied evidences of its increase and prosperity—the contrast of what had come with what had gone.

In 1829 he was appointed by Sheriff-Principal M'Neil—afterwards Lord Colonsay—to the office of Sheriff-Substitute at Dunblane. His appointment to such an office at the early age of thirty is a proof of the reputation he had already achieved. It may be believed that the change from the active duties of a profession, and the stir of a large city, to the comparative repose of the judicial bench in the little cathedral town was at first somewhat trying to him. Yet he had learned, wherever he was, to find employment. He soon showed, and he never ceased to take, an interest in the history of the beautiful district where his lot had thus for a time been cast; while the further professional study in which he was enabled to engage, and the judicial experience gained during this short season of quiet, must have been a valuable preparation for the duties of the important position awaiting him. In the autumn of 1833, he was promoted to the office of Sheriff-Substitute at Perth, which he held for half a century, and in which, as has been remarked, "he won for himself a name and fame of national dimensions."

The duties of the Perth Sheriff Court are of no light order. A multiplicity of cases comes before it. But Sheriff Barclay, in dealing with them, never failed to exhibit the highest judicial qualities, combined with his inborn activity and vigour. His work was never in arrear. His decisions commanded confidence, and were rarely reversed. His relations with the members of the local bar were of the kindliest description. And his abilities were shown not only in his conduct of the business of the Court, but likewise in the valuable law treatises which he published. These dealt most successfully with various matters of interest, while the chief of them, his "Digest of the Law of Scotland," etc., took its place as a standard work. The University of Aberdeen marked their sense of its value by bestowing on him the well-merited degree of LL.D.

It has been said of him in this connection by one whose opinion is well worth recording, "His reputation as the lawyer and judge rests upon too solid a basis for ephemeral appreciation. His books on jurisprudence have long been acknowledged as storehouses of reliable information, and safe guides in practice, while his able and exhaustive judgments showed how he could blend the rigorous exercise of law with the sound dictates of common sense. His judicial notes, chaste and elegant in diction, sparkled with epigrammatic sallies ; and in reading them one was apt to forget that the stern realities of litigation were involved in the elucidation."

But by the community generally Dr. Barclay, while honoured as a judge, was regarded rather as a friend and benefactor. Naturally and rightly so. For he was ready unto every good work, helpful in every worthy cause. A warmly attached member and office-bearer of the Church of Scotland, he was always willing to be associated with the members of other churches in deeds and offices of Christian charity and philanthropy. No request for his aid in the furtherance and advocacy of what promised to be of service to his fellow-men was refused, if he could possibly meet it. While his practical wisdom was of much avail in the guidance and direction of the various benevolent institutions in the city, his presence on the platform at the friendly conference or re-union was eagerly solicited and joyously welcomed. He was ready, felicitous, and eloquent of speech, with the telling anecdote or illustration ever at hand to give force to what he said. Of abundant humour, it was a humour never caustic or capable of causing pain to others, but genial, bright, and kindly. His meeting with the pupils of the Sabbath, public, and Industrial Schools—of which last he had from their commencement been a steadfast advocate and supporter—were invariably most happy and successful. He was always — what active men often fail to be—in sympathy with the young His voice, beyond that of any other, had a charm and cheer for them. They felt that out of the abundance of the heart he spake to them. Yet not less happy was he in speaking to older people —whatever the special form in which he sought to benefit them—whether by conveying instruction or salutary counsel. Many of the addresses which he delivered on social and other matters have been given to the world in more permanent form.

 He took great pleasure in the study of Biblical subjects. He did not claim to have made original investigations—his busy life did not admit of such a thing—but he had read much and widely in connection with them. The results of his reading were often set forth in such lectures as are here reproduced. No doubt some of the conclusions to which he had been led, and which at the time were held to be well established, may appear less certain in the light of later research ; but he never failed to show clearly what, as he apprehended it, was the actual state of a question or controversy. And the mere printed page can furnish but a faint idea of his ability and success in lecturing, of his liveliness and tact, of his skill in arresting and securing attention, and of the increased interest which, by means of the remark or observation of the moment, he imparted to what he had written. These things live in the memory of those who were privileged to listen to him.

It may be added that expression was in various ways given to the feelings cherished towards him, and to the sense of the valuable services he had rendered. On the 22nd Dec., 1868, at a large meeting presided over by Lord Kinnaird, Lord Lieutenant of the county, he was presented with his portrait, painted by a distinguished artist, while a handsome presentation of plate, &c., was made to Mrs. Barclay. On completing his jubilee as a sheriff, he was entertained to dinner in the County Hall—the chair being occupied by Lord Adam—and received numerous congratulatory addresses. And it was felt after all that these and other tributes were but faint recognitions of what was due to one, who had set such an example of integrity, diligence, and unselfishness.

In October, 1883, after a rather severe illness, and by advice of his medical, and other friends, he resigned his judicial office. It was remarked at the time that he was "the oldest member of the Glasgow Faculty, the oldest Sheriff-Substitute in Scotland, and the oldest judge in Britain." He himself recorded that it had been "his great privilege to co-operate with ten Sheriff Principals ; that he had known fourteen successive Lord Provosts of Perth ; that he had lived during the reign of four sovereigns, and had the honour, on 14th June, 1837, of proclaiming at the cross of Perth, the accession of Her Gracious Majesty Queen Victoria." It was fondly hoped that when freed from the duties and responsibilities of office, he might still be spared for a little while. Nor did the expectation seem unwarranted. He had made a favourable recovery. He had resumed as if with increased energy and relish, many of his labours of beneficence. He was also meditating the republication of several of his earlier works and addresses. But on Saturday, the 25th January last, he was seized with paralysis, and gradually became weaker, until on the 1st February he peacefully passed away— having just completed his 85th year.

The intimation of his death was received with deep regret throughout the country. In the city where he had so long dwelt, every heart was touched as by a sense of personal loss. His remains were borne to the grave amid manifold and touching tokens of respect, and sorrow. He had filled a place all his own. He had been to those that knew him what no one else, in their day, could be.

# HEATHEN MYTHOLOGY: CORROBORATIVE OR ILLUSTRATIVE OF HOLY SCRIPTURE.

## I. THE CREATION.

LET us in imagination go to the summit of some alpine height, whose lofty peak looms far in misty outline, on which rests the first dawn of rising sun, and which receives the last ray from its ocean bed. There, from some flinty rock, struck not by Hebrew Prophet, but by the Almighty Creator of heaven and earth, wells forth a crystal spring. Now it glides silently down the declivity, then leaps from rock to rock, or slowly meanders amidst mossy banks enamelled with many and lovely flowers, blushing unseen to human eye, "wasting their sweetness on the desert air." Reaching the valley it assumes the distinctive character of a stream, and gains a name, still moving onward with rapid pace, or with sluggish wave. It may divide itself into separate channels, again to be united with increased volume ; other lesser streams pay tribute to its majesty, and pour their liquid contributions into its accumulated current. For a while some such streams refuse to mingle their waters, and for a distance may be distinguished by their colour. The river for a time may disappear underground, again to issue to the light of day, or be held back in the expanse of inland sea ; here it may issue forth with altered name and character, and pent up between giant rocks ; or there it may leap the mighty cataract, and surge in the gigantic whirlpool underneath. Some rivers are more extended in their course, and pass through many kingdoms, and divers tongues are spoken on their banks. Often they form provincial boundaries, and too often in the world's eventful history have their waters been crimsoned with blood in cruel and often vain attempts of aggrandisement or encroachment by the powerful on the territory of the weak. Finally, however, let their course be long or short, direct or tortuous, they all reach the ocean. Some enter it with such a mass of waters as in themselves form a sea ; others by several mouths empty their stores into the great cistern of waters. One character they have in common. Their origin is on *land*, and their final termination is *sea*.

" Time writes no wrinkle on thine azure brow.
Such as creation's dawn beheld, thou rollest now;
\* \* \* \* \* \* \*
Thou glorious mirror, where the Almighty's form
Glasses itself in tempests."

The parallel may be easily drawn in the history of mankind. Men of philosophical minds, too often gainsaying the holy book of Revelation, have written much about several centres of creation, and thereby have sought to explain the varieties of the human species. But laying aside, for the moment, the divine authority for the unity of race and common origin of humanity, there is no tradition to support such crude imaginations, and all such theories are exposed to far greater and more formidable objections than the simple Scripture testimony they vainly attempt to supersede.

The common tradition in favour of unity of race is supported by eminent philosophers and physiologists. All seeming objections, arising from variety in the species, assuredly will be, if they have not already been, overcome by the patient investigations of the learned. By certain eminent men the diversity of race has been supposed to have had its origin at the dispersion at Babel, when the Creator, not merely by the confusion of tongues, but by some physical change of body, fitted the dispersed tribes to dwell in different climes. This theory is so far supported by the fact of humanity falling under three great divisions, answering to the three sons of Noah, whose names are held to indicate white, red, and black. In like manner Sir William Jones and other philologists trace all diversity of languages to three distinct sources—Sanscrit, Arabic, and Slavonic, or Tartarian. By a school of anthropology all changes have been ascribed to the gradual operation of climate and the long-continued oppression by one race of other kindred races, it having pleased the great Creator, doubtless for wise and most benevolent purposes, to dye the skin of the one with a darker tint or a yellower shade than others of more favoured climes.

The traditions of mankind trace humanity up to one common source from which have been derived, in many streams, the nations of earth; some for a time of slender numbers and of small repute, others in mighty volume; some mingled and lost with other nationalities, or now progressing with the slow advance of peace and anon with fearful revolutionary leap. One nation, or rather "peculiar people," has alone for ages preserved its identity as the "People of God"; scattered and peeled amongst the nations, it has never ceased to maintain its peculiar characteristics, and doubtless is upheld as the amalgam, which in God's own time is once more to render mankind one in faith as they are one in blood, when there shall be

> "One land, one home, one friend, one faith, one law :
> Its Ruler, God—its practice, righteousness—
> Its life, peace ; for the one true faith we pray :
> There is but one in heaven, and there shall be
> But one on earth, the same which is in heaven."

We proceed to inquire whether, in the traditions of heathen mythology, there are to be found statements in harmony with the divine record of the creation and fall of man. Now these statements are found in nations far remote from what may be called "the land of the Bible," and in records so ancient that they could not be derived from the Jews or their sacred writings. As might be expected, they are uniformly mixed with the alloy of human imperfection, distorted and disfigured according to the vain imagination of fallen humanity. They are not seen in the clear mirror of Scripture record, but as if through the prism of man's unsanctified reason, often separating what God had put together, and colouring the pure light of heaven, according to the taste or fancy of His erring creatures. How gracious in God to provide for His Church and people "a sure word of prophecy" "as a lamp to our feet and a light to our path."

On the primal fact of creation the Mosaic record

is short and simple. Enough to satisfy him who, by *faith*, is assured that " *God created the world,*" but leaving nothing to gratify idle curiosity or encourage perplexing inquiries. Fuller in his " Marvels of Science" has truthfully said, " Without this history the world would be in total darkness, not knowing whence it came, or whither it goeth. In the first page of Genesis a child may learn more in one hour, than all the philosophers of the world learned without it, in a thousand years. The Mosaic narrative, while describing the grand incidents of the creation, is less a *history* than a *religious exercise*, apprising us that all things had a beginning, and that beginning was with God. It shows us our origin and our mission, and points out in precise and unmistakeable terms the debt of worship, obedience, and service which we owe to our Maker. The work of creation receives but a cursory glance, just to set forth the supremacy of its Author; but the history of *man*, to whom addressed, is related at large, and the various epochs of his career are faithfully and carefully noted. In short, the account given by Moses is a lesson not in *science* but in *religion*, appealing by its simple dignity to the understanding, while it carries conviction to the minds of the enlightened and the wise."

The introductory sentence in the Bible announces the great fact, "In the beginning God created the heavens and the earth"; or, as it is said, the original might have been better rendered, "the *substance* of the heavens and the earth." The existence of God is assumed, and that He was the Creator is declared. A *beginning* is affirmed, but *when* that was is veiled as much as when shall be the end. Then follows the simple announcement, "The earth was without form and void (or rather invisible and unfinished), and darkness was upon the face of the deep; and the Spirit of God moved upon the face of the waters (or abyss)."

We now turn to heathen mythology, and select a few from the many traditional statements of Cosmogony, or the generation of the world. The oldest writings extant, except Holy Scripture, are fragments of the books of Sanchoniatho, who is thought to have lived before the Trojan war, or from ten to twelve centuries before Christ. This ancient writer records the opinions of the Phœnicians as to the creation thus—"The beginning of all things was a dark and confused windy air, or a breeze of thick air, and a chaos turbid and black, and these were unbounded, and for a long series of ages destitute of form." We next quote from Berosus, who wrote from records preserved in the temple of Belus at Babylon : " There was a time in which there existed nothing but darkness and an abyss of waters." In the Laws of Manu which contain the mythology of Hindostan, it is said that " The universe existed only in the first divine idea, yet unexpanded, as if involved in *darkness* undiscoverable by Reason and undiscovered by Revelation, as if it was wholly immersed in sleep. But the self-existing power, having willed to produce various beings from his own divine substance, first with a thought created the waters." " He framed the heaven above and the earth beneath ; He gave birth to time and the divisions of time, to the stars also and to the planets." The following passage is from the *Vedas*, or the four oldest books of the Hindoo religion :—" The Supreme Being alone existed ; afterwards there was a universal darkness; now the watery ocean was produced ; then did the Creator, Lord of the Universe, rise out of the ocean, and successively framed the sun and moon, which govern day and night, whence proceed the revolutions of years." In Persian mythology, their god *Ormuzd* created the world in six different intervals of unequal endurance, but the whole amounting exactly to a solar year; and the subjects of creation in each successive period nearly coincide with the Mosaic account, especially that man was made in the sixth period.

It will be thus seen that, in all these references, chaos, darkness, water, and light followed precisely in the order of the Mosaic narrative. Similar extracts might have been given from Gothic and Scandinavian traditions, and from the writings of Hesiod, Aristotle, Orpheus, Plato, Ovid, and other ancient authors. We cannot close these corroborative evidences without alluding to the wild ravings of a modern school, which denies the existence of a Creator, but maintains the theory of evolution, thus falling far short of anything like a sensible solution of difficulties. We extract a few sentences from one of the most eminent leaders of the materialistic school—Professor Lorenz Oken of Zurich. In the strange and transcendental language of the Professor, "The eternal is the nothing of nature. There exists nothing but nothing—nothing but the eternal. God is a rotating globe. The world is God rotating—the whole universe is material—is nothing but matter, for it is the primary act repeating itself eternally on its centre. The universe is a rotating globe of matter; there is no dead matter, it is alive through its being—through the eternal that is in it. Matter has no existence in itself, but it is the eternal only that exists in it. Everything is God that is there, and without God there is absolutely nothing. Everything that is, is material. Now, however, there is nothing that is not, consequently there is everywhere nothing immaterial." Moleschott, another of the same school, writes, "Man is produced from wind and ashes. The action of vegetable-life called him into existence. Thought consists in the motion of matter; it is a translocation of the cerebral substance. Without phosphorus there can be no thought, and consciousness itself is nothing but an attribute of matter." Czolbe, also of the materialistic school, describes man as being nothing more than a mosaic figure made up of different atoms, and mechanically combined in an elaborate shape. The words of Socrates might be well applied to such unmeaning language: "All is quite dark and obscure by the unassisted light of nature, and we never can attain to certain knowledge save by a revelation from Him who cares for us."

II. DIVISION OF TIME—THE SABBATH.

IN the Mosaic record each section or division of time is thus announced: "And the evening and the morning was the day." There need be no difficulty in respect of the word "day," used as language of accommodation. Let it ever be remembered that the word is used with regard to God, with whom "one day is as a thousand years, and a thousand years as one day." As darkness preceded light, the natural mode of reckoning is from darkness to light. The Jews accordingly, in whatever part of the world they are cast, observe this primeval reckoning, especially with regard to their Sabbath, which they reckon from sunset on the Friday night until sunset on Saturday. This reckoning is not confined to the Jews. It was adopted by the refined Athenians, as well as the barbarous Goths in the forests of Germany, and also by the Celtic nations. Even with ourselves, though adopting another reckoning, we use the same language, recognising the ancient division of time. Our modern reckoning from twelve o'clock noon to the same hour at midnight is entirely arbitrary, and depends on no natural phenomenon. On whatever hour of the day we make an appointment, or convene a meeting—if on the week following, we say "se'night" or seven nights; if on the second week, we use the term fortnight, or fourteen nights.

A strong confirmation of the authenticity of the divine record is to be found in the universality of the seventh or Sabbath day. Simple is the divine record, and beautiful in its simplicity. "On the seventh day God ended His work which He made, and He rested on the seventh day from all the work which He made; and God blessed the seventh day, and sanctified it." Every other division of time is regulated by celestial phenomena observable by our senses. The day is marked by the alternation of darkness and light, according to the diurnal rotation of the earth on its axis. The month is equally recognised by the lunar courses. Indeed, the word "moon" signifies, the measure, as is still more apparent in the Latin term "*mensis*." The year is fixed by the revolution of the earth around its central orb with its succession of seasons. But the seven days division depends solely on positive or arbitrary law ; and it never could have entered into the mind of man to invent this seventh division of time. It must have come down in the stream of time. "We find," writes Goguet, "the use of this period among all nations without any variation in the form of it. The Israelites, Assyrians, Egyptians, Indians, Arabians, and all the nations of the East have in all ages made use of a week consisting of seven days. We find the same custom among the ancient Romans, Gauls, Britons, Germans, the nations of the North, and of America." From the fact of the seventh epoch being the completion of the great work of creation, the number seven in all languages has been held to be the figure of completion or perfection. Not only in Scripture is it thus symbolized. Hesiod declares that the "seventh day is holy." Homer writes, "Then came the seventh day—that is sacred;" and at another place, "It was the seventh day, wherein all things were finished." Linus, a Greek poet, repeats the same sentiment: "The seventh day is among the best things; the seventh day is the nativity of all things; the seventh is amongst the chief; and the seventh is the perfect day." Callimachus writes, "In seven all things were perfected, in the starry heavens which appear in their orbs throughout the rolling year." Eusebius writes, "Almost all the philosophers and poets acknowledge the seventh day as holy." Plato records "the seventh day as a festival to every nation." Josephus affirms, "No city of Greek or barbarians can be found which does not acknowledge a seventh day's rest from labour." Piazzi Smyth, the Astronomer-Royal, has found in the Pyramids of Egypt traces of a sevenfold division of time, with the seventh specially marked. Even the nomenclature of the heathen, still affixed to the days of the week, bears evidence of the sanctity of the seventh day as being set apart for the worship of their principal deity—*the sun*. All physiologists are agreed that both to man and beast occasional rest is an absolute necessity, and what is required is a seventh day. The lately-deceased Bianconi, who had the largest stock of horses in Ireland for carriage, by resting his enormous stud on Sabbaths, proved that the endurance of their lives, and their fitness for labour, were greatly enhanced in comparison to others who refused to give their animals the same indulgence. He is reported to have said, " I have always found by giving my horses rest on the Sunday I have got more work out of them, and saved, at least, twelve per cent. at the end of the year by giving the horses as well as the men a Sunday's rest." We have an opposite fact. When France, under the blasting influence of infidelity, worshipped Reason as God in the person of a profligate woman, and wrote " No God " on its churches, and " Death an eternal sleep " on its cemeteries, with blind consistency it endeavoured to blot out all traces of religion by substituting a *tenth* instead of a *seventh* day's rest. In vain did the votaries of infidelity strive to cancel this relic of paradise and antepast of heaven. Let Britain read the sad result, and tremble if she dares to tread the same fatal path. The reign of terror ensued. Men became fiends. The fields of France were steeped in blood. The Sabbath of the *seventh* day was foremost in heralding in more peaceful times. May it not still be matter of grave reflection whether with regard to that fair but unhappy country its disregard to the holy Sabbath, making it a day of politics and pleasure, has not some connection with its disasters from without, and dissensions within? Their political assemblies and amusements are chiefly held on Sabbath, and almost all their defeats in recent wars were sustained on the Sabbath. How striking the comment on the text, "Him that honoureth Me I will honour." We are sorry to find in our own country the same practice prevailing—having mass meetings on the Lord's day ; and the great cry, countenanced in influential quarters, is to have museums and all public places open on Sabbaths as well as week days. It is worthy of remark, that the only two grand institutions which we can trace to Paradise are marriage and the Sabbath. No observing person can look to passing events but must remark, that of all institutions these are the two which are chiefly made the objects of attack by the infidel and the secularist. It has been truthfully as well as beautifully said, " The Sabbath is the golden clasp which binds together the volume of the week."

We desire to dwell somewhat more at length on the two Edenic ordinances, which have come down to our time, and will assuredly endure (rudely assailed though they now are) until the end of this world. These are the divine institution of the Sabbath and the holy ordinance of matrimony. As to the latter, on marriage depends the growth and prosperity of nations with their moral and spiritual wellbeing. It is gradually passing from the sphere of a *sacred* and *religious* ceremony into a mere *civil* contract. No longer is the intention " or purpose of marriage" solemnly proclaimed in the house of prayer, in time of public worship. A mere notice is given on a street-board in the same way as all manner of soft and hard goods are exposed for sale by public roup, or intimation made of dogs being lost and found. Instead of the ceremony being celebrated in church, as uniformly required in England (and by the Directory of public worship, equally required in Scotland), it may now be performed at any time and at any place. Indeed, the ceremony may be transacted by the parties themselves without the interference of minister or magistrate. No longer is it viewed as a *divine* and *religious* ordinance whereby the parties become one, united in every interest until death parts them. It is not now the maxim, " What therefore God hath joined together let not man put asunder." The marriage union is viewed somewhat in the light of a mercantile partnership, or joint-adventure, or as forming a connection of master (or it may be mistress) and servant. The forbidden degrees announced in Holy Writ are scoffed at and endeavoured to be set aside by Act of Parliament. Not being married in *the*

*Lord*, and without a divine blessing on the union, what sad results follow! We cannot read our daily newspapers without mournfully perusing accounts of wife-beating, and often wife-murder. Desertions and elopements of one or other of the spouses and neglect of their offspring are only too frequent occurrences. Not long ago an Act of Parliament was requisite in England to obtain a divorce which was only within the reach of the rich. Now, a court in England has been instituted for divorce cases. In Scotland we read of the vastly increasing number of divorce suits in our Court of Session, in which all ranks and classes of society are included. It has nearly come to this, that a man may, as in ancient times, give a bill of divorcement to his wife and put her away. So, too, children say to their aged parents, "Corban, it is a gift by whatsoever thou mightest be profited by me." Instead, as in ages gone by, of children being proud to venerate and support their aged parents, they frequently cast them on the cold mercies of the Poor-Law Board, and leave them to terminate their days within the walls of a poorshouse.

On the Sabbath question a united attack is now made on that holy day, and we regret to discover in the ranks of the foemen those calling themselves Christians—nay, Christian ministers. In all large towns numerous shops are open, and traffic proceeds as on secular days. Political and mass meetings are held on that blessed day of rest. Already in *our* streets on the Lord's day youths, and men too, are engaged in the gambols and sports of the week. Not long since in Glasgow a body of police making a foray on a party playing foot-ball in the public green, and capturing the object of play, found to their horror that it was a human skull. It could not have been its fitness for the sport, as it wanted elasticity. It seemed to show their derision of death, and mockery alike of mortality and immortality. The present movement is not for the opening of mission-churches and halls, but for the opening of museums, libraries, picture-galleries, and gardens. The plea for this inroad on the Sabbath is to raise the taste of the masses. It is easy to see that those who would frequent these resorts are men whose tastes are already refined, and who *can* and *do* visit them any week day. Nothing but the Gospel can raise mankind from sin and misery and uplift them to the higher sphere of intellectual, moral, and spiritual culture. Should the movers succeed in their limited attempts to secularize the hours of the Sabbath, we must expect, at no distant period, the opening of the theatre, circus, and dancing-saloon inevitably to follow. These will be more attractive to the masses, and assuredly will tend more to degrade than to elevate the population. Large meetings of the anti-Sabbatarians have been lately held. At a meeting in Glasgow, numbering some thousands, an eminent scientific professor had the hardihood to deny that Christ is the "Lord of the Sabbath." He announced, without contradiction, that man is "Lord of the Sabbath," and so may change it to the Monday or abolish it altogether if he choose.

We are not of the number who view the Sabbath as a day of gloom only to be celebrated by a solemn dirge. It is a day of peaceful *joy*, because it proclaims "Christ is risen." It is a day of rest from *worldly* employments, but a day of *work* of the highest enjoyment. The true Christian, instead of finding it a weariness, finds it pass too swiftly, and that he has not gained time for all the sacred and spiritual work he desired to have accomplished.

One word to the sons of toil and labour:—Listen not to the siren strains of those who would rob you of your Sabbath under pretence of being your friends. Depend upon it they will give you a *stone* for *bread* and a *serpent* for a *fish*. If they succeed, it will be that seven days' work will be exacted for six days' wage. It will be worse than Egyptian bondage. The tale of bricks will be demanded, but the straw wherewith to burn them will be denied, and the labourers left to provide fuel for themselves. Bishop Bickerseith has beautifully and truthfully remarked, " There is but a step between the never hearing a Sabbath-bell, or never entering a church, or never joining in public worship, and being confirmed in irreligion." Another author has well observed, " The Sabbath is God's special gift to the working man, and one of its chief objects is to prolong his life and preserve efficient his working tone. It replenishes the spirit, the elasticity, and vigour which the last six days' work have drained away, and supplies the force which is to fill the six days succeeding, and in economy of existence it answers the same purpose as, in the economy of income, is answered by a savings bank. The savings bank of man's existence is the weekly Sabbath." Another author has said, " He who forgetteth the Sabbath of the Lord is on the highway to forget the Lord of the Sabbath." Just as prayer maketh a man give over sinning, so sinning makes a man give over praying. Philip Henry well remarked, " Oh, if a well-spent Sabbath be not heaven, it is assuredly the way to it." Old Herbert has beautifully as well as truthfully written—

" O day, most calm, most bright !
The fruit of this, the next world's bud,

> The indorsement of supreme delight,
> Writ by a friend, and with his blood,
> The couch of time, care's calm and bay,
> The week were dark but for thy light ;
> Thy torch doth show the way."

### III. THE GARDEN OF EDEN.

THE Mosaic record states very briefly that man was made "after the image of God"—a holy and happy being. Every previous act of creation was attributed simply to God. Before the future tenant of the fair creation is made, a divine council is held, and "God said, Let us make man in our image." Each act of creative power is summed up with the divine approval, "God saw that it was *good*." But when the final one was completed the superlative is added, "And God saw *every* thing that He had made, and, behold, it was *very* good."

Then it is recorded, "The Lord God planted a garden eastward in Eden ; and there He put the man whom He had formed," "to dress it and keep it." It thus seems that man was not formed in Eden, but put or placed therein to test his obedience. God then pronounced to him as the simple rule of life, "Of *every* tree of the garden thou mayest *freely* eat: but of the tree of the knowledge of good and evil, thou shalt not eat of it; for in the day that thou eatest thereof thou shalt *surely* die." The restriction is evidence at once of the sovereignty of the Creator, and the free will and responsibility of the creature. The Scripture proceeds to record, that man, deceived by the devil embodied in the serpent, violated the commandment, forfeited his high destiny, incurred the penalty of death at once spiritual and corporeal, and was therefore "sent forth from the garden of Eden, to till the ground from whence he was taken." But, at the same time, there was given the promise of redemption, in that "the seed of the woman should bruise the head of the serpent (or devil)." We are led to the belief that this the first promise of the Saviour was fully made known to the original pair. This is shown by the early sacrificial lamb offered by Abel, and the declarations of Scripture, that Christ Jesus was "*the* lamb slain from the foundation of the world."

All nations of antiquity have a tradition of a golden age, followed by one called the iron age. Berosus represents the life-blood of Divinity to have been incorporated into the body of the first man; and he adds, "On this account it is that mankind are rational and partake of divine knowledge." The Hindoo mythology represents that

"God having divided His own substance, His mighty power became half-male and half-female."

Adim, according to Sir William Jones, in Sanscrit means "the first." The Persians give the name Adamah to the first man. Sale states that this word in Persian means "red earth," which forms a singular coincidence with the Mosaic record that man was made from the earth, and that at death "he was to return to the ground, for out of it was he taken : for dust he was, and unto dust should he return." Indeed, our own English words "human" and "humanity" have the same analogy from *humus*, the ground. The like root is found in the name Esau and Edom. The sacred record of man's origin—both corporeally, or from the dust, and spiritually—is reconcilable with reason. "And the Lord God formed man of the dust of the ground, and breathed into his nostrils the breath of life ; and man *became a living soul*." Fearfully and wonderfully was man formed. The spiritual essence came directly and immediately from God. So, too, Jesus, before He left this earth, "breathed on the disciples, and said, Receive ye the Holy Ghost." The truth is shown in the common language of every nation, and in our own vocabulary in such words as "inspire," "expire," "inspiration," and such like.

How defiant of reason, and how repugnant to all authority or tradition, the wild speculations of the development scheme, which traces creation to the whirl of atoms in space, and man, in his origin, to the molluscs or sponges—reaching the penult stage in the monkey and gorilla, and which refers all mental efforts to the action of phosphorus, similar to the *ignis fatuus,* or "will of the wisp," of the marsh.

The garden of Eden finds place in the traditions of all ancient nations. Subsequent portions of Scripture bear immutable evidence of a garden or grove having been the original seat of man. "Abraham planted *a grove* in Beersheba, and called there on the name of the Lord the everlasting God." In progress of time, however, as shown by the same traditions, heathen nations planted groves, and made them the temples of false gods, and scenes of cruel rites. Hence the oft-repeated commands to cut down the groves of the vanquished nations. The Jews were commanded "not to plant a grove of any trees near unto the altar of the Lord their God." The prophets repeatedly denounce the grove worship of the Gentile nations. Isaiah especially is very pronounced on this—"They shall be ashamed of the oaks which ye have desired, and ye shall be confounded for the gardens that ye have chosen." With a very obvious allusion to Eden, the prophet speaks of those "who sanctify themselves and purify themselves in the gardens *behind one tree in the midst.*" Strabo, the heathen historian, records that "all sacred places, even where no trees were to be seen, were nevertheless called groves." Hence the "Academic grove." Indeed, light and grove have a common parentage—hence the saying, "*Lucus a non lucendo,*" interpreted to mean "light from darkness," though strictly meaning "the grove without light." Arab legends discourse of a garden in the east, on the summit of a mountain of Jacinth, inaccessible to man—a garden of rich soil and equable temperature, well watered, and abounding with trees and flowers of rare colours and fragrance. There is a Hindoo tradition that "in the middle of the seven continents of the Puranas is the golden mountain of Meru, which stands like the seed-cup of the lotus of the earth. On its summit is the vast city of Brahma, renowned in heaven and encircled by the Ganges, which, issuing from the foot of Vishnu, washes the lunar orb, and falling thence from the skies, is divided into *four streams* that flow to the *four corners* of the earth. In this abode of Divinity is the grove of Inda; there, too, is the *Jambu* tree, from whose fruits are fed the waters of the Jambu river, which gives life and immortality to all that drink thereof." The Chinese have a tradition of "an enchanted garden on the summit of a high chain of mountains farther north than the Himalaya. The fountain of immortality, which waters these gardens, is divided into *four streams*—the fountains of the great spirit Tychin." The Zend books mention a region called *Heden*, and the place of Zoroaster's birth is called *Hedenesh*. The four rivers in two of these traditions form a very striking coincidence to the four rivers mentioned in the *Mosaic* account, and one of which is still known in the east, and again appears in the last portion of Holy Scripture. The purpose of this strange mention of river names may have been intended to show that the place of probation was on earth, and not, as was once supposed, that man like the apostate angels had been cast out from heaven. The Bible students cannot but be led to the description of heaven in the Apocalypse, with "its pure river of water of life, and on either side the tree of life, which bare all manner of fruits; and the leaves of the tree are for the healing of the nations."

Philostratus mentions that there was a Phœnician colony at Cadiz, where there was a beautiful garden, in which were two peculiar trees. No female was allowed to enter that garden, because of some tradition that with her sex was the origin of evil. It had a temple guarded by lions, and three altars to Poverty, Manual Labour, and to Hercules or the Saviour. The garden of the Hesperides is a beautiful illustration of the Mosaic record. That garden was said to have been surrounded by high mountains, and could only be entered by the Son of the High God. The golden apples, which hung on a mysterious tree, were guarded by a nymph, with the aid of a Dragon or Serpent. Hercules, the deliverer, killed the Serpent, and carried away the apples, but not without the aid of Atlas, who was fabled to bear the heavens on his shoulders. Hercules sent Atlas to bring the apples, and in the meantime undertook the task of supporting the heavens. A group of ancient statuary recovered from Rome represents a tree with rich fruit hanging thereon, and a serpent intertwined among the branches, and Hercules seated under them between two nymphs.

Our own country still has the traces of grove-worship in the Druidical circles. These temples were surrounded by thick groves where human sacrifices were offered in the vain attempts to expiate sin. The very name Druid is derived from the oak; and the mistletoe, so essential to Christmas festivities, is a parasite of the oak. The

Christmas tree proclaims the ancient belief that man's fall and restoration were intimately connected with a tree, which in its latter view bestows varied gifts on man. When Christianity superseded the rites of the grove-worship there were not wanting memorials of these on Gothic architecture. The cathedral with its lofty roof, its gigantic pillars, leafy capitals, interlaced windows, admitting "a dim religious light," are all reminiscences of the ancient grove.

A very striking tradition of the creation and fall of man is given by J. G. Kohl in " Kitchi-Gami, or Wanderings around Lake Superior," translated in 1860. He mentions the following singular traditions amongst the Red Indians :—" The first man and woman were placed in a garden rich with all manner of fruit. They ate, and lived there for days and years in pleasure and happiness : and the Great Spirit often came to them, and conversed with them. 'One thing,' He said, 'I warn you against. Come hither. See, this tree in the middle of the garden is not good. In a short time this tree will blossom and bear fruits which look very fine and taste very sweet, but do not eat of them, for if you do so you will die.' One day, however, when the woman went walking in the garden she heard a very kindly and sweet voice say to her,

'Why dost thou not eat of this beautiful fruit? It tastes splendidly.' She resisted for some time. The voice was repeated. The fruit smelled pleasantly, and the woman licked it a little. At length she swallowed it entirely, and felt as if drunk. When her husband came to her soon after she persuaded him also to eat of it. He did so, and also felt as if drunk. But this scarce had happened ere the silver scales with which their bodies had been covered fell off; only twenty of these scales remained on, but lost all their brilliancy —ten on the fingers, and ten on the toes. They saw *themselves to be quite uncovered, and began to be ashamed, and withdrew hurriedly into the bushes of the garden.*"

### THE FORBIDDEN TREE OR FRUIT.

THERE is a wide-spread tradition, existing in most countries, to the effect that it was an apple which was the object of temptation and the occasion of the fall of man. Indeed, there are some who have persisted in alleging that Scripture itself declares that very fact.[1] There are certainly strange hints in common language of some such authorized reference to this peculiar fruit. "The apple of dis-

[1] It is somewhat remarkable that the Romans should have a word for "*apple*" and "*evil*" not greatly unlike.

cord" is a well-known phrase. The "apples of Sodom," which find place in Holy Writ, and are not unknown in Syria, are received tokens of sin and vanity. Anatomists as a class may not always have been under the influence of Scripture, yet from all antiquity a certain protuberance on the throat has received from them the name of "*Pomum Adami*," or the Apple of Adam, as if the deceptive fruit had been difficult for our first parents to swallow. In the valuable collection of hieroglyphics published by the Egyptian Society, and edited by Dr. Thomas Young, there is a *fac-simile* of a tablet found in the Temple of Osiris at Philæ, which must have been of an age *anterior* to the era of Abraham, and therefore long before the publication of the Pentateuch or books of Moses. On this tablet there is represented the whole scene of the temptation and fall. The tree is exhibited—the man and woman stand by, with the fruit in their hands—the serpent erect and winged, and not as now on its belly. Above the tree is the unmistakable word "The Pomegranate." The beauty of this fruit may be inferred, from the description given in the Encyclopædia Britannica, which could have been written with no theological tendency. "The *Granatum* or common pomegranate rises with a tree stem, branching numerously all the way from the bottom, growing eighteen or twenty feet high, with spear-shaped, narrow, opposite leaves, and the branches terminated by *most beautiful*, large red flowers, succeeded by large, rounded fruit as big as an orange, having a hard rind filled with soft pulp and numerous seeds." Dr. Thomson, in his admirable volume " The Land and the Book," in describing the pomegranate, says, " The fruit is as sweet to the taste, as it is pleasant to the eye." There could not have been a more direct and yet undesigned reference to the description given in Genesis of the fruit of the tree of knowledge of good and evil—" good for food and pleasant to the eyes." One remarkable fact is, that both the ball-shaped flowers and the fruit are of a blood-red colour, so much so, that it was used by the ancients to dye scarlet, and even in modern times it gives the tinge to morocco leather. The Egyptians used the pomegranate as an essential in their funeral rites. The most remarkable fact is the oft-repeated reference to the pomegranate in Scripture imagery, as well as its actual place in the Temple furniture and the priestly garments. Even in the wilderness, where the tree had no place, Moses was commanded to frame the golden candlestick as an emblem of the Church of the future. It was surrounded with knops and flowers. " A knop, under two branches of the same "—this repeated three times—" according to the six branches going out of it, their knops and their branches were of the same; all of it was of one beaten work of pure gold." It is agreed, that the knops were pomegranates. Then, when ancient Israel had fixed their dwelling in the Land of Promise, and the Temple was erected and richly furnished, the chains which ornamented the two great pillars had one hundred pomegranates; and four hundred pomegranates were interwoven with the wreaths which surrounded the chapiters of the pillars. So with the robe of the priesthood. "The robe of the ephod was to be *all* blue (the emblem of purity from the vault of heaven), and beneath, upon the hem of the robe, the command was to have pomegranates of blue and of purple, and of scarlet round about the hem thereof, and bells of gold between them round about—a golden bell and a pomegranate—a golden bell and a pomegranate upon the hem of the robe round about." These may have been a fitting forecast or type of sin and salvation—the fall and recovery—Paradise lost and Paradise regained. If the apple and pomegranate have thus been received popularly as emblems of the fall and consequent sin, so equally have people acknowledged flowers and bells to be tokens of salvation and of the resurrection. Bells have ever been in use to call people to the House and worship of God, and flowers were often the burden of prophecy and the theme of our Redeemer, and still are in many churches made use of for decorations. Bells have, in the cause of superstition, been consecrated and baptised. So flowers are invariably received as tokens of the resurrection, and are frequently strewn on the coffins and graves of the departed.

Dr. Mason states that the Karens, inhabiting the mountains and valleys of the interior of Burmah, have traditions of the Creation, the temptation, the fall, and the dispersion of nations, both in prose and verse nearly identical with the narrative given in the Bible. We give a portion bearing on the section of which we are now treating. "In ancient times God created the world. All things were minutely ordered by Him. He appointed the fruit of trial. He gave minute orders. Satan deceived two persons. He caused them to eat of the fruit of trial. When they ate the fruit of trial, they became subject to sickness, old age, and death. Had they obeyed and believed God, we should not have been subjected to sickness; we should have prospered in our doings. Had they obeyed and believed Him we should not have been poor."

The Scripture student cannot but notice the coincidence of the temptation offered successfully to our first parents, and again, but unsuccessfully, by the same Tempter to the second Adam. Both were threefold—"good for food, pleasant to the eyes, and to make one wise." "The lust of the flesh, and the lust of the eyes, and the pride of life" (1 John ii. 16). In the case of our divine Redeemer these were presented *separately* and much more intensified, and under circumstances where resistance seemed likely to be much less strong than in the case of our first parents. The grant was most ample—"Of *every* tree of the garden thou *mayest freely* eat." The restriction was the slightest—but guarded by most *express* sanction of death. "But of the tree of the knowledge of good and evil thou *shalt not* eat of it, for in the day that thou eatest thereof thou shalt surely die." It is well to remark the seductive art of the Tempter. His words were not at the first a denial of the restrictive grant, but merely a question of curiosity to induce doubt. The woman, in listening to the voice of the Seducer, gave the opportunity. She artfully restricted the grant by striking out the words "*every*" and "*freely*"; and as mankind still are doing, she increased and intensified the restriction by adding the words, "neither shall *ye touch it*," and instead of the positive penalty, "thou *shalt surely* die," the penalty is modified into the *probable*, still clung to by many in modern times, "*lest* ye die." The Tempter, emboldened by the tokens of success, at once assumes the character of "liar from the beginning, and father of it," by the bold assertion, "ye shall *not surely* die."

## THE SERPENT.

THE Serpent, in ancient as well as in modern times, has been held as having some intimate and mysterious connection with the introduction of sin into the world and the fall of man. The animal is repeatedly noticed in Scripture as the arch enemy of God and man—the old Serpent. God appearing in the burning bush first sealed the commission to Moses by his rod being transformed into a serpent, and re-transformed to the rod, which afterwards was the symbol of power in dealing with Pharaoh, and which was still made use of by the modern necromancer. The same miracle was the first wrought by Moses before the haughty monarch of Egypt, but which his magicians (Jannes and Jambres amongst the chief) were enabled by some mysterious agency to imitate. Serpents were sent as the instruments of punishment on the idolatrous Israelites in the wilderness, whilst, at the same time, an image was held up as the object of recovery through faith, and by the Redeemer shown to be typical of Himself. "And as Moses lifted up the serpent in the wilderness, even so must the Son of Man be lifted up." The very symbol, in after times, was, in its turn, made by the Israelites an object of idolatrous worship. The brief account of the fall sets forth that "the serpent was more *subtile* than any beast of the field which the Lord God had made." Our divine Redeemer gives the animal as the emblem of wisdom. A power was given to the apostles to overcome serpents, and, in exercise of that power, the apostle to the Gentiles in Melita or Malta, with ease threw the viper which had fastened on his hand into the fire. In heathen eyes he was at once raised from being suspected as a murderer to the character of a god. So, when we turn to heathen mythology and tradition, we find the serpent continually introduced. The Egyptians made it an object of worship, whilst with other ancient nations, it was held as the type of the evil principle. In some of the tablets in the temple of Osiris in Egypt, there are frequent representations of serpents. Captain Fraser thus describes a tablet found on one of the tombs of the kings in ancient Thebes: "Eve stands in parley with a serpent, and next to her stands a god with a sharp arrow piercing a serpent's head." In another tablet, copied by Sir Gardiner Wilkinson, is a woman who thus pierces the head of the serpent. In ancient mythology Bacchus was worshipped as the first planter of trees and gardens. On his festivals his image was placed on a car drawn by lions, leopards, and other beasts of prey, in obvious allusion to the original subjection of all animals to the supremacy of man. The attendants were accustomed to carry serpents, and to shout in jubilation, "*Evoe! Evoe!*" In the temple of Apollo at Delphi every seventh day was a festival in which the priests chanted a hymn in honour of the serpent. In the temple of Belus at Babylon there was an image of the goddess Rhea, and near her were very large serpents in silver, thirty talents each in weight; and an image of Juno, holding in her right hand the head of a serpent. Mercury, the messenger of the gods, had two serpents entwined around his caduceus or wand. Æsculapius, the god of physic, had a staff which a serpent embraced, and that animal is still the armorial sign of the medical profession. The three Furies, whose duty it was to scourge the wicked, had snakes twisted in their hair. Serpent-worship existed in the religion of the Persians and Brahmins. The dragon is the standard of the Chinese, and the same honour is given to that animal in Japan. The coins of ancient

Tyre have the same effigy. The serpent had a place in Druidical worship, and has been found in the Indian idolatry of Central America. In every country there are found legends of mighty serpents with deeds of bloody cruelty, and places are still marked as dragons' caves and dragons' dens. The Church records prove, that on certain days people were wont to visit such places, and to propitiate the supposed being who held mysterious power in the district. So, too, some of our most noble families have traditions of being ennobled because of their slaying some dragon, the terror of the vicinity. Saint George of England won his spurs and his saintship by the slaughter of a mighty dragon. We must observe that the animal, as now seen, is under the curse, eating dust and moving on its belly. It is said by scholars that the words Seraph, Serpent, and Satan all own the same root, denoting that they are winged creatures, and so the serpent may have been at the time of the temptation. It is to be presumed that the arch enemy of man would for a time assume the form most suitable by its beauty for the purpose of seduction. The serpent is above all animals now hated, shunned and destroyed by man. Concealed in herbage (the "snake in the grass") the heel of man is the object of its venomous attack, while the life of the animal seems to be in its head, which is the object of man's attack in destroying his assailant. It is undoubted that the animal possesses some mysterious mesmeric power, which has at some distance an influence through its eyes to bring birds within its grasp. Scripture refers to serpent-charmers. These are well known in India, and by the power of music bring serpents from their holes, and by some mysterious power grasp and capture them in the manner that the rat-catcher prosecutes his calling in other regions. A returned missionary from India has narrated, that on one occasion, when a party was assembled, a little child was left to enjoy itself on the floor of the bungalow. The mother's attention became directed to her infant playing with some object projecting from the wall of reeds. The mother, on approaching her child, was terrified to find the little one playing with the head of a large deadly *cobra*, whose body was concealed within the reedy wall. A more apt illustration of the sacred text could scarcely be found than such an incident, illustrative of Gospel times, when " the sucking child shall play on the hole of the asp, and the weaned child shall put his hand on the cockatrice's den " (Isaiah xi. 8).

## THE CREATION AS EXEMPLIFIED IN THE GREEK AND LATIN CLASSICS.

HITHERTO we have selected traces of traditions relative to creation, existing amongst ancient and uncivilized nations, far distant from what is known as the "land of the Bible." We now gather the like traces from the classics of the more modern and civilized nations of Greece and Rome. It is often noticed, that Palestine, in respect of its central situation, was admirably suited for sounding throughout all the earth the glad tidings of gospel salvation. The Old Testament record was entrusted to the Jews, and their language was one little familiar to others; but situated as they were in so advantageous a position between the eastern and western hemispheres, there can be little question that they became the instruments of divulging the sacred truths first intrusted to them as to the creation of this globe, and of man, its temporary occupant. Perhaps, for the like end, the captivities of the Israelites were designed by the Almighty for still farther carrying truth into distant parts of the earth. It cannot be supposed, but that Daniel and his companions left their impress on the people of Babylon, and that all were made to feel that God was with them, and the only true

God. Still more, when under the wonderful counsels of Providence, the Hebrew books, hitherto much of a sealed record, were in Egypt translated into Greek—then the most common language in the world—the learned of all nations eagerly sought to enrich themselves with the ample stores of history, to be found nowhere else. The Septuagint, translated from the Hebrew about 280 years before the birth of our Saviour, helped in many ways to make known His advent.[1] It was from such information that the wise men of the east learned the time of the birth of Him who was to be the Saviour of the world, and also the region of His birth. It may be here remarked, that such facts as that of Greek being the adopted version of the New Testament, and the derisive inscription over the Cross of Jesus being set forth in three languages, as well as the miracle of tongues on the day of Pentecost, appear to proclaim that the gospel was no longer confined to the Jews, but was for "all people that on earth did dwell." It is not to be wondered at, therefore, that the learned men of Greece and

---

[1] The translation received the name of Septuagint because, according to a wide-spread tradition, seventy-two learned men were said to have been engaged on the translation from Hebrew to Greek.

Rome eagerly sought out the salient points of the Mosaic record, and worked them up with their debased mythology, and their multitudinous deities, whose names, like that of the Evil One himself, were legion. Their number indeed was so great, that there was a division into superior and inferior, and the latter were so numerous that they had to be classified into divisions. Orpheus reckoned the number of superior deities alone at 365. But Varro enumerated 300 Inferiors, and Hesiod computed 30,000 deities hovering above the earth in the air. Paul thought it not unworthy of his noble argument on Mars Hill, to quote, from the hymn of Cleanthes to Jupiter, evidence that their own poets confessed that man was made in the image of God. The ease with which men were made to pass from the region of the terrestrial into that of the celestial, is seen by the barbarians of Melita (Malta), when they viewed Paul at one moment as a murderer, but in the next looked upon him as a God; or when Paul and Barnabas were at Lystra, the people, because of the miracle done on the cripple, "lifted up their voices, saying, 'The gods are come down to us in the likeness of men;' and they called Barnabas Jupiter, and Paul Mercurius, because he was the chief speaker. Then the priest of Jupiter brought oxen and garlands unto the gates, and would have done sacrifice with the people." Scholars have remarked, that the 4th eclogue of Virgil to Pollio, is a literal translation of various passages of Isaiah.

The Supreme God, by the ancients, was held to be "father of gods and men"; by the Greeks called Zeus (God); by the Romans Jupiter. It is worthy of remark, that the proper name Jupiter appears incapable of regular declension, and crops out in the genitive as *Jovis*, a direct recognition of the Hebrew *Jehovah*. The Greeks recognised three divinities united into one Supreme God. Thus both the Greeks and Romans gave appellations to the Supreme Deity, answering very nearly to the attributes ascribed in Scripture to the true God—especially "Optimus Maximus"—the Best and Most High. "Jupiter Tonans" or the thunderer, was his prerogative and favourite appellation, hence a thunderbolt or flint stone were the symbols of his power. In the words of Job, "God directeth His voice under the whole heaven, and His lightning into the ends of the earth. After it a voice roareth: He thundereth with the voice of His excellency; and He will not stay them when His voice is heard. God thundereth marvellously with His voice; great things doeth He which we cannot comprehend." In both Greece and Rome, Jupiter was represented as "determining the course of all human affairs." He foresaw the future, and the events happening in it were the results of his will (Smith's Classical Dictionary). As Lord of heaven, white was his colour, white animals were sacrificed to him, white horses drew his chariot, and his priests were arrayed in white.

Pandora bears a very remarkable likeness to mother Eve. She was supposed in the classic age to be the *first woman* on earth. When Prometheus had stolen fire from heaven, Zeus, in revenge, caused his son Vulcan, the god of fire, "to make a woman out of earth, who by her charms and beauty should bring misery upon the human race. One god adorned her with beauty, another bestowed upon her boldness and cunning, and so she was called Pandora, or 'the All-gifted,' as each of the gods had given her some power by which she was to work the ruin of man" (Smith). She became the wife of Prometheus. In his house there was a closed jar or box, which he by Zeus was forbidden to open; "but the curiosity of woman could not resist the temptation to know its contents, and when she opened the lid, all the evils incidental to humanity poured out and spread over the earth. She had only time to shut down the lid and prevent the escape of *Hope*." There can be no better recognition of the fall of man than this with its accompanying woes, but still with the hope of salvation, to be accomplished by the seed of the woman in the fulness of time. Vulcan, the god of fire, and of smiths, obviously has its root from Tubal Cain, omitting the first syllable and changing the *b* into a *v*, not uncommon in ancient languages, and thus we have the Scripture name. So too, Achilles, invulnerable all but the heel, because held by his mother when plunged into the river Lethe, in order to render him proof against all weapons of warfare. We shall only add amongst many other recognitions of Scripture in the Roman Pantheon, some slight allusion to Hercules, by the classics supposed to be the saviour of man. Hercules being the son of Zeus or Jupiter, consequently was the *Son of God*. On the day of his birth, his father boasted of his becoming the father of a hero who was to rule over the nations. A hostile god sent two serpents to the cradle of the child to destroy him, but with his infant hand he strangled both. The twelve labours of this imaginary deity are often recognised in classic pages, and amongst these are the destruction of a lion, the hydra, and many other monsters. The purification of the Augean stables, or rather byres, with the accumulated filth of 3000 oxen for 30 years, by diverting a river to sweep them clean, is one of his greatest achievements. This allusion would almost lead to the conclusion, that much of the character of this imaginary divinity was founded on portions of the prophecy of Isaiah, foretelling the glory of gospel times. The strangest part in his drama of life is, that having by an enemy been poisoned by a garment which stuck to his skin and exposed him to excruciating pain, he voluntarily laid himself on a pile of wood and desired it to be set on fire. "When the pile was burning, a cloud came down from heaven, and amid peals of thunder, carried him to Olympus, where he was honoured with immortality" (Smith). Were it not undoubted that these delusions were received and embalmed in poetry, long before the advent of our Redeemer, they might have been supposed to have been written after His advent and ascension. Infidel writers have been anxious to convert the book of Isaiah from prophecy into history, and to assign its date, at least the date of the later portion, to a recent period. But there is, in any case, ascertained evidence of the Evangelical prophet having written his book centuries before the birth of the Redeemer.

Before leaving this section dealing with the Creation, we may shortly notice some evidence derived from the signs of the Zodiac and the constellations. So much did this appear, that Volney and Dupuis, two leading French infidels, while acknowledging the fact, argued that mankind had taken their theology from the starry vault of the firmament, and not that the firmament was the impress of revealed theology. It is not surprising that in early ages, when written records were unknown or scanty, mankind should symbolize great truths in the canopy of the heavens. So in the words of the Psalmist, " The heavens *declare* the glory of God, and the firmament *sheweth* His handiwork; day unto day *uttereth speech*, and night unto night *sheweth* knowledge. There is no *speech* nor *language* where their *voice* is not heard. Their *line* is gone out through all the earth, and their *words* to the end of the world." Accordingly, in the Book of Job, the most ancient portion of the Bible, there is a distinct recognition of constellations, by the very names under which they are known in modern astronomy. The Pyramids of Egypt bear unmistakeable evidence of astronomical science in the world's early youth. The Chinese and other nations have distinct records of eclipses and comets, remote in pre-historic times. The stars which form a constellation do not at once give the figure, but require lines to be drawn from one star to another, thus grouping them together. *Libra* is thus made to symbolize *the justice of God*. *Scorpio* is death.

*Sagittarius* represents the conqueror of death in the figure of Scorpio. *Hercules,* or the Saviour, is represented as treading on a dragon's head. *Capricornus* represents the sacrificial goat. *Aquarius* is the symbol of the Holy Ghost poured out as water. *Pisces,* the fishes, has always been the symbol of the Church. Similar symbols may be found in the blessings of Jacob on his twelve sons, as recorded in the 49th chapter of Genesis, especially *Leo* in the *Lion* of the tribe of Judah. *Virgo* has often been recognised as a wonderful symbol of the Christian creed. Though prostrate on the ground, her high estate is shown by her having wings. She holds in one hand ears of corn, emblems of the chosen seed; in the other hand she raises the *palm* of future victory.

There is an apparent solemn, yet delightful analogy between *Paradise lost* and *Paradise regained,* for thus saith the Scriptures, " By *one man* (the first Adam) sin entered into the world, and death by sin, and so death passed upon all men, for that all have sinned. For as by one man's disobedience *many* were made sinners, so as by the obedience of *one* (the second Adam) shall many be made righteous." Our high estate was lost in a garden, *Eden.* It was mainly regained in a garden, *Gethsemane.* A *tree* was the chief instrument of the loss—the tree of good and evil. A tree was the chief centre of salvation—the cross of Christ. At the crucifixion the serpent—the devil—was permitted for a time to bruise the heel of the seed of the woman, but, blessed be God, Jesus forever bruised the head of the enemy of God and man. The earth had been cursed for man's original sin, "thorns and thistles" did it thereafter yield; but even the earth seemed saved from the curse, thorns being made the crown of our Redeemer. It was, indeed, by sinful men placed in derision, but by God it was the palm of victory over sin and death. The river, issuing from Paradise parted into four streams to water the earth. In the new earth there is one river, "the pure river of the water of life, clear as crystal, proceeding out of the throne of God and of the Lamb." In Eden there was only one tree of life, with but another, the tree of knowledge of good and evil; but in the heavenly paradise there is no tree of knowledge of good and evil, for evil is unknown, and temptation has no longer power. The only knowledge is to know Christ, whom to know is life eternal. In the new Jerusalem there is symbolized in the midst of the street, and on either side of the river, the tree of life, which bore twelve manner of fruits, and yielded her fruit every month, and the leaves of the tree were for the healing of the nations.

> "A fairer Paradise is founded now
> For Adam, and his chosen sons, whom thou
> A Saviour art come down to reinstall
> Where they shall dwell secure, when time shall be
> Of tempter and temptation without fear."[1]

So sung Milton, but still more graphically did Pollok sing in his "Course of Time," Book II. :—

> "Man sinned; tempted, he ate the guarded tree,
> Audacious, unbelieving, proud, ungrateful,
> He ate the interdicted fruit, and fell;
> And in his fall, the universal race;
> For they in him by delegation were,
> In him to stand or fall, to live or die.
>       . . . . . .
> "That Jesus, Son of God, of Mary born
> In Bethlehem, and by Pilate crucified
> On Calvary, for man thus fallen and lost,
> Died; and, by death, life and salvation bought,
> And perfect righteousness, for all who should
> In His great name believe.
>       . . . . . .
> "To God, to Him that sits upon the throne
> On high, and to the Lamb, sing honour, sing
> Dominion, glory, blessing sing, and praise!
> When man had fallen, was ruined, hopeless, lost,
> Messiah, Prince of Peace, Eternal King,
> Died, that the dead might live, the lost be saved."

[1] "Paradise Regained," Book IV., 613-617.

## THE DELUGE.

THE drama of this eventful world may appropriately be divided into three stupendous acts. The first terminated with the deluge. The only authentic record of this is to be briefly found in three chapters of Genesis. With the deluge the curtain rises on the second stage of the world's existence. Mankind was again limited to a single family, from which source were to flow out anew the diversified nations of the earth. With Ararat commenced the second great epoch of humanity, and it closed with the scene of Gethsemane and Calvary. The passage from the first to the second exhibits a stupendous display of divine justice, yet mingled with mercy to the faithful few. The transition to the third has still the element of justice, but far surpassing that is the wondrous proclamation of love and mercy to sinful and fallen man, at once fulfilling and magnifying the law and making it honourable. We are all actors in this the final scene of the world's history. We are assured that it shall likewise terminate. The curtain shall finally descend to rise on a new and better because a perfectly holy world, without termination, " world without end." The *when* may be guessed, but with the wise characteristic of Scripture prophecy the exact date has been, and is likely ever to be, matter of doubt and dispute. The ancient advice is still a sound one, that would-be prophets should protract the fulfilment of their vaticinations beyond the likely period of their own lives, lest they live to experience the foolish rashness of their soothsaying. Our natal day is to us the genesis of the world, and our death its doom. Our last day is to us the last of time, in which our connection with this fleeting world is for ever dissevered.

> " Trust no *future*, howe'er pleasant ;
> Let the *dead* past bury its *dead*.
> Act—act in the *living present*,
> Heart within and God o'erhead."

As might reasonably be expected, the traditions of the deluge are found to be more minute and widely diffused than those of the creation of the world and the fall of man. The account of the Edenic expulsion must have come down from sire to son until it reached the little crew of the ark. The longevity of the antediluvian race rendered the links in the chain of communication few in number. We are apt greatly to miscalculate the number of generations between two points of ancient history. Ask any man suddenly how many generations existed between the creation and the deluge ; or again, from that event till the birth of Christ ; and once more, from that blessed event till the present time; or from any historic event in the world's history until to-day;—it is likely that the person so asked unintentionally will give a far greater number than on severer thought will be found to be the fact. We especially are apt to measure the term of man's existence in antediluvian times by the limited threescore and ten, the span of life in later ages. The long term of life allotted to the antediluvians may have been designed to afford easy transmission of facts, before their reduction into written records, as well as to advance the plan of the Almighty of multiplying the human race. It, however, affords sad evidence that long life, if not spent in holiness and the service of God, becomes a curse instead of a blessing. We have the fact that there was but one link between Adam and Noah and his sons. Methuselah was a contemporary of Adam for many years, and of Noah for a nearly equal number. The traditions of the fall came down to Moses through only six persons —Methuselah, Shem, Abraham, Isaac, Joseph, and Amram. Illustrative of the erroneous measure of time often assumed we may give some modern instances. Some few years ago there was a well-known citizen in Glasgow, aged 88, known from his writings as to ancient Glasgow by the name of

*Senex.* His fellow-citizens invited him to a banquet, and it was noticed in the public papers at the time, that if his ancestors, who were a long-lived race, had severally attained his age, the twenty-second of the upward series must have been in life before the Christian era. So it may be mentioned that the writer of this paper, when himself a boy, has often conversed with persons who remembered in their childhood the rebellion of 1745. He, when a boy, knew an aged man, then a highly-respected ironmonger in Glasgow, who, when an apprentice smith, was compelled, in 1736, to use a sledge-hammer to break open the door of the Heart of Mid-Lothian or Edinburgh Jail, that Captain Porteous might meet his doom at the hands of the murderous and mysterious mob. From his participation in the riot the young lad had to leave Edinburgh and thereafter make Glasgow his abode.

It may be well to notice that Scripture frequently makes reference to numerous records now regarded as unnecessary since the sure word of prophecy has been given in its entirety and integrity. There are upwards of twenty references to books and records now lost or unknown, though we are not without hope that through the researches now in progress in the east, some vestiges of these may be found. Thus the fifth chapter of Genesis clearly refers to a prior record commencing "This is *the Book* of the generations of Adam." Indeed, some eminent biblical scholars, from internal evidence, are of opinion that the first four chapters of Genesis were the work of Adam or Seth. There is the radical change of the name of the Almighty from God to the Lord God. In the same way the narrative of the deluge may first have been recorded by Noah himself, or Shem, and repeated by Moses. The oft-repeated "these are the generations" point in that direction. These suppositions receive no small corroboration from precise quotations given by Jude of the prophecies of Enoch, the seventh from Adam. Whether language was a divine gift of God or of human invention, it cannot but be believed that mankind, at an early age, acquired the art of recording passing events. We find that there were instructors of "every artificer in brass and iron," and in "handling the harp and organ," and even the art of poetry is found in the lament or dirge of Lamech. We can scarcely suppose but that some mode of perpetuating events must have existed before the deluge.

Before entering into the fertile field of heathen traditions, it may be well to notice how frequently the great fact of the deluge is referred to in Scripture itself. Our belief in this, therefore, does not rest solely on the brief account given by Moses. It is once referred to by Isaiah (chapter liv. verse 9), twice by Ezekiel (chapter xiv. verses 14 and 20). Our Divine Redeemer recognises the fact on two occasions (Matthew xxiv. verses 37-39, Luke xvii. 26, 27); the Apostle Peter refers to it three times; and Paul, or the inspired author of the Epistle to the Hebrews, once (chapter xi. 7).

So many and so various are the references to the deluge in the traditions of nations, that, amongst the multitude, it is difficult to select. We shall commence with the *Pantheon*, or the Deities of ancient nations. It is apparent that the chief origin of idolatry was hero-worship. Men who had long and wisely filled a principal place in the history of a people were naturally, in the estimation of their fellow-countrymen, supposed to be alive in some semi-exalted state of being, still interested, and with greater power to operate, in the matters they had left behind. So, on the intercession of their former countrymen, they were supposed to exercise power to protect and regulate the affairs of kingdoms. In this way we are enabled to trace the person of Noah amongst the Deities of antiquity. He appears as Osiris, Typhon, Bacchus, Saturn, Uranus, Deucalion, Minos, Janus. These rank in the first or chief class of

Divinities, and that among nations far distant the one from the other alike in space on the world's surface as in the tide of history.

*Osiris*, the chief God of ancient Egypt, was so named as "*the many-eyed.*" His symbol was an eye and a sceptre, emblems of omniscience and omnipotence. *Typhon* was represented as having formed an ark or coffer of beautiful workmanship. He invited Osiris to enter—Typhon shut him in and threw the ark on the sea, but it was cast ashore by the waves. *Bacchus*, when attacked by his enemies, took refuge on the sea, where, according to some traditions, he was miraculously preserved by a Sea Deity, but, according to other traditions, his life was preserved in *an ark*. He afterwards taught men to cultivate the vine, the leaves of which always form the chaplet of his image. He also educated men to manufacture the juice of the grape, which would have been well, had it ranked amongst the unknown or lost arts, as truly then "ignorance would have been bliss." *Saturn* and his wife *Rhea* were born on the ocean. Hence a ship has ever been his symbol. He is also represented as the common parent of mankind. He had three sons, Jupiter, Neptune, and Pluto, amongst whom was divided the earth. To Jupiter was assigned the land, to Neptune the sea, and to

Pluto the region of the lost. The Egyptians styled one of his sons Ammon, who it was said made his old father drunk with honey mead, and in that state bound and mutilated him. Scripture readers will here recognise the reference to the mysterious deed of the father of Canaan. *Deucalion* was preserved in an ark, from which he sent out a dove to discover if the waters had abated.

The recognition of the fact of the Deluge is to be found in the names, rites, and temples of the Pagan world. The Temple of Osiris was at *Theba*, or *Thebes*, in Egypt. *Theba* is the Hebrew name for ark. In the religious ceremonies of this deity, a ship formed the prominent object, and was carried about in religious processions. From Herculaneum there has been recovered a picture of a female carrying on her shoulders a square box of a remarkable shape. The word denoting ark occurs frequently in ancient classics—either as *Chelos* —*Kibotus*—*Arca*—*Larnax*. It is remarkable that in Scripture the word rendered *ark* in the sixth chapter of Genesis, only occurs once again, in recording the ark of bulrushes which hid the infant Moses, who was to be the deliverer of his people. In the sacking of Troy, Eurypylus had an ark, which contained the image of Bacchus. On attempting to look into the secret chest he was struck blind. An obvious reference to the people of Bethshemesh for a like impious curiosity. There is extant an ancient coin struck in the reign of Philip the Elder, in the city of Apamea, in Phrygia, which anciently was called *Kibotus* or the ark. On the reverse is represented a square machine floating on water, and inside a man and woman. Two birds are seen, one has in its bill a small branch of a tree, underneath there are three Greek letters, N O E. Though this has by some scholars been disputed, yet Faber, Horne, and Taylor agree in the letters.

We proceed to select passages from ancient heathen writers regarding the Deluge. The earliest record extant is the Chaldean, copied by Berosus from the archives of the Temple of Belus at Babylon. He writes—"Chronus appeared to Xionthius in a vision, and warned him that upon the fifteenth day of the month Dæcius there would be a flood by which mankind would be destroyed. He enjoined him to build a vessel and take with him into it his friends and relations, and everything necessary to sustain life, together with the different animals, both birds and quadrupeds, and trust himself fearlessly to the deep. After the flood had been upon the earth and was in time abated, he sent out birds from the vessel, which, not finding any food nor any place whereupon they might rest their feet, returned to him again. After an interval of some days he sent them forth a second time, and they now returned with their feet tinged with mud. He made a trial a third time with these birds, but they returned to him no more, from whence he judged that the surface of the earth had appeared above the waters."

Our next quotation is abridged from Lucian, an ancient Greek writer—" This generation, and the present race of men were not the first, for all those of that former generation perished. But these are of a second race, which increased from a single person, named *Deucalion*, to its present multitude. The men were of a violent and ferocious temper, and guilty of every sort of lawlessness, therefore a great calamity befel them. The earth suddenly poured forth a vast body of water, heavy torrents of rain descended, the rivers overflowed their banks, and the sea rose above its ordinary level, until the whole world was inundated, and all that were in it perished. In the midst of the general destruction Deucalion alone was left to another generation on account of his extraordinary wisdom and piety. Now this preservation was thus effected. He caused his sons and their wives to enter into a large ark which he had provided, and afterwards went into it himself. But while he was embarking, swine, and horses, and lions, and serpents, and all other animals that live upon the face of the earth, came to him in pairs. These he took in with him, and they injured him not, but on the contrary the greatest harmony subsisted between them through the influence of the Deity. Then they all sailed together in one ark so long as the water prevailed."

In one of the sacred books of the Parsees there is the following passage—" The world having been corrupted by Ahriman, the Evil One, it was necessary to bring over it a universal flow of waters, that all impurity might be washed away. Accordingly the rain came down, in drops as large as the head of a bull, until the earth was wholly covered, and all the creatures of the evil one perished, and then the flood gradually subsided; and first the mountains, and next the plains appeared once more." Similar passages have been translated by Sir William Jones from the first Purana or sacred book of Hindostan. The ancient records of China have the like allusion to a great catastrophe, wherein it is said, " The earth fell to pieces, and the waters enclosed within its bosom burst forth with violence and overflowed it."

On this section of our subject we add passages from Ovid, the Roman poet, who died in the 17th year of the Christian era. He describes the flood at great length, as sent by Jupiter in vengeance on a wicked race. He describes the ruin caused by the waters in these words :—

> "The bearded corn beneath the burden bends,
> Despondent clowns deplore their perished grain,
> And the long labours of the year are vain."

The escape of Deucalion is thus recorded :—

> "A mountain of stupendous height there stands
> Between the Athenian and Bœotian lands,
> The bound of fruitful fields, while fields they were,
> But then a field of waters did appear;
> High on the summit of this dubious cliff
> Deucalion wafting moved his little skiff;
> He with his wife were only left behind,
> Of perished man, they two of human kind.
> The most upright of mortal man was *He*,
> The most sincere and holy woman *She*."

We have given several traditions, collected from many ancient nations, in corroboration of the brief Scripture record of the deluge or flood. The most cogent of all is of recent discovery, and amounts to something like an actual record rather than tradition, and recorded many centuries before the era of Moses. It has been matter of thankfulness, that when men of eminence vainly seek to attack the divine record with "science, falsely so-called," the

Divine Author of the Word has in mercy opened up a rich and almost inexhaustible store-house of corroborative evidence of pre-historic facts. Nineveh and other ancient cities have been disentombed from their slumber of ages, and disclose new and irresistible proofs of the facts briefly recorded in the divine page. The statement we are about to make as to a record of the flood was some time ago first announced to a large public meeting of the Bible Archæological Society held in London. The distinguished Sir Henry Rawlinson was in the chair, and men of the greatest eminence in philosophy and science formed the audience. The Essayist was the profound antiquarian, the lately deceased Dr. George Smith of the British Museum. His subject was " On a Cuneiform inscription describing the Deluge." The lecturer, in the course of examining many tablets brought from Nineveh, with great labour and pains, from their fragmentary nature, and the difficulty in deciphering them, at length discovered a full though distorted record of the Flood. There have been a vast number of tablets or cylinders discovered in the ruins of the Royal Palace in Nineveh, and amongst the number, though somewhat mutilated, was a record of the Deluge. It was obvious from many allusions, that some of these records were not *originals*, but "*squeezes*," or transcripts of still more ancient tablets. Occasionally the copyist has remarked, "Here the original is defective." The lecturer, with others skilled in such lore, had come to the decided conclusion that the originals were of a date coeval with Noah, and probably had been written by himself, or under his direction, during the 350 years of his life, after the Flood. In Genesis x. 10, we read of the city of Eroch—by Ptolemy it is called Orchæ, and now is known as Warka. It undoubtedly owed its erection to Nimrod, who flourished 2,000 years before Christ, or 4,000 years ago. Between Nineveh and Eroch, in the days of their greatness, there must have been much intercourse. The Royal Library of Nineveh, it is thought, possessed no fewer than 20,000 of these ancient records engraved on tablets of baked clay. These tablets are fortunately of a much more enduring material than ancient manuscripts or modern books. In the opinion of those best able and entitled to judge, several of them are held to be reprints of more ancient records. If the Nineveh record be taken as the date, we have evidence of the great event of the deluge recorded upwards of 3,000 years ago. Or if we go back, as eminent archæologists declare we are entitled to do, then not less than forty centuries have passed in the world's history since the fact was originally recorded on those tablets. Dr. George Smith, aided by other eminent archæologists, has with great labour first put in entirety the broken fragments of tablets and then deciphered these ancient records. It is obvious that the task has been faithfully performed, but it is also apparent that in the copy a difficulty had been found even by the Nineveh transcribers, and still more by Dr. Smith and his compeers. It will thus appear that sentences are not completed, and chasms are left in their structure. It is also shown that even in the early era of Nineveh the mythology of the heathen had to some extent forced itself into history. We must therefore acknowledge with gratitude to God, that at a later period of time, under divine guidance, Moses gave for all time a "sure word," without unnecessary details, but enough to record the salient points of the great event, its object, and results.

As to the general outline of the details of the history as obtained from these broken cylinders or tablets, it is recorded in detached sentences—1st, That the Gods spake to a man and said, "Make a great ship for thee and I will destroy the sinners and life."—2nd, That "He was to cause to go in the seed of all life to preserve them.—3rd, "The vessel was to be 600 cubits in length, 60 cubits in breadth and height."—4th, "He was to pour bitumen over the outside and inside."—5th, "He fixed an altar for offering—oxen were slaughtered."—6th, "All my male and female servants, the beasts of the field and the animals of the field, I caused them to go up."—7th, A flood came in the night; "I will cause it to rain heavily from heaven." "I entered into the midst of the ship and shut the door." "A storm arose from the horizon of heaven extending and wide." "It thundered, we went over mountains and plains, the flood reached the heaven. Bright earth was to a waste turned, all life was destroyed: brother saw not brother."—8th, On "the *seventh* day was a calm, the storm and all the tempest quieted. The sea He caused to dry, and the tempest ended. The whole of mankind like reeds,—their corpses floated. I opened the window and the light broke in. I sat still and over my refuge came peace."—9th, "To the country of Niser went the ship, the mountain of Niser stopped it. On the *seventh* day I sent forth a Dove and it left and went, and a resting-place it did not find, and it returned." I sent forth a swallow, and it left but returned. I sent forth a raven and it left. The corpses it saw and did eat, and swam and wandered away. I sent forth the animals to the four winds.

I poured out a libation, I built an altar on the peak of the mountain.—10th, " When His judgment was accomplished, Bel went up to the ship, He took my hand and brought me out, He caused to bring my wife to my side. He purified the country. He established in a *covenant*, and took the people."— 11th, " He said the cry of the man alarms—this do, this *scarlet* cloth place on his head, and the day he ascended the sides of the ship, his wife placed the *scarlet* cloth on his head."

After the essayist had given other numerous extracts from the records, of which the preceding are only a few, he proceeded to show how far these coincided with, or disagreed from, or were supplementary to, the brief but sacred record given in Genesis. The records agree—1st, That the sinfulness of man was great.—2nd, That the flood was sent as a punishment for sin.—3rd, That a man or a family were saved in a ship.—4th, That the man was directed to construct the vessel according to measurements.—5th, That it had only one door and one window.—6th, That it was pitched without and within.—7th, The *seventh* or Sabbath day was recognised.—8th, The ship rested on a mountain.—9th, Birds were sent out to discover if the waters were abated.—10th, An altar and sacrifices were established in the ark, and again, on being delivered therefrom,—facts not recorded in the sacred volume, but extremely probable.—11th, A *covenant* was made on the delivery. There are several remarkable incidents introduced in the tables which do not appear in Genesis, such as the saved few setting up stones in commemoration of the awful judgment, which very likely had reference to the tower of Babel. The scarlet cloth, typical of the blood of atonement, is a remarkable feature in the tables, especially when it is again found as the token of safety to Rahab, the saved of Jericho, from destruction in a future age. There are some minor discrepancies between the human and divine records, but which only tend to show how speedily tradition becomes vitiated, and the natural inclination of humanity to exaggerate and distort events, to suit its proud and vain imaginations.

The essayist closed his observations with remarking that " This account of the Deluge opened a new field of inquiry, on the early part of the Bible History. The Cuneiform inscriptions are now shedding new light on many questions, and supplying material which future scholars have to work out. It would be a mistake to suppose that, with the translation and commentary on an inscription like this, the matter is ended. Beneath the mounds and ruined cities of Chaldea, now awaiting exploration, lie, together with older copies of this Deluge text, other legends and histories of the earliest civilization of the world."

The chairman (Sir Henry Rawlinson) guaranteed "the accuracy of Dr. Smith's translations. He wished to explain to the meeting, that, although the tablets found in the ruins of Nineveh dated only from the age of Sardanapalus in the 8th or 7th century before Christ, yet they were copies of much more ancient documents."

Mr. Gladstone (Premier) made a speech of great weight. In moving a vote of thanks to Dr. Smith he remarked, "We are like children with an enormous pattern map broken up into a thousand pieces, in which the ingenuity and learning of men like your President, and Vice-President, and the gentlemen here to-night, by degrees, ascertain the proper spot for this or that particular fragment, then after a time another is added to the first discovered, and so we go on point by point, until at last, I believe, the result will be that we shall be permitted to know a great deal more than our forefathers have known, with respect to the early history of mankind, and perhaps the most interesting and the most important of all portions of the various history of our race, with reference to the weighty interests which are involved either for science or even for religion."

Attention may here be called to an unfinished paper in a number of the "Life and Work" magazine. It is from the pen of the late Dr. Robert Jamieson, of Glasgow. That distinguished clergyman had long devoted his time and talents to Oriental studies. In this fragment, so far, Dr. Jamieson narrates the successful labours of Dr. George Smith, but unfortunately death prevented Dr. Jamieson from completing his treatise. He argues that the date of the broken Monhush tablet is at least 2,000 years before the birth of our Redeemer, and that has been ascertained to be a fragment of a Chaldean account of the Deluge.

There are two questions connected with the deluge which have long been the subject of dispute amongst eminent scholars, and which, so far from being yet satisfactorily settled, we believe never in time will be solved. The first question is, whether the deluge was *partial*, and limited to some eastern section of the world, or whether it was *general*, encircling the whole of the terrestrial globe? The second question is the particular mode of operation, whether general or partial, by which the flood was produced? It will be admitted that the solution of either question is nowise essential to divine revelation—the grand and sole object of which is man's salvation through a Redeemer. It must ever be recollected that the Bible was not given to teach science, or any other department of mere human knowledge. We have formerly quoted the words of an eminent author—" That the narratives given by Moses are lessons not in science but in religion —less a *history* than a *religious exercise.*" The Archbishop of York, in his Bampton lectures, observed that "in religion God has given us truths not to satisfy our *reason* but to guide our *practice.*" The late Professor Crawford, speaking of the mysteries of revelation, well observed " that the system, like the constitution and course of nature, is a scheme *imperfectly* comprehended by us, and consequently that some things contained in it may seem to our limited minds not easily reconciled, but which, did we more thoroughly know, might be found to be *perfectly* consistent with the divine perfections."

All we have to learn from the divine record is the *fact* of the deluge, be it general or partial. The *fact* remains the same in either way, and is likewise wholly independent of its mode of operation. The frequent use in the Scripture record of the deluge, as well as in its other historical details, of the well-known figure of speech (*synecdoche*), where the whole is taken for a part, and general terms are made use of, merely to denote the greatness of particulars, is readily admitted. Taking the *end* and *object* of the event, there can be no reasonable doubt that the *means* would be commensurate with the *end;* yet, as with all the works of the Almighty, without any waste of power or work of supererogation. Unnecessary expenditure and complexity of power is often characteristic of man. Simplicity and economy are characteristic of all the works of God. If, then, the sinful race of man were at that early age of humanity co-extensive with the world, we would with all humility consider the deluge to be equally co-extensive, so as to effect its object. But if the range of the sinful population were circumscribed, so might the remedy be equally limited, and in either way the truthfulness of the divine record be wholly undisturbed. In support of the *general* theory we have such distinguished scholars as Drs. Hamilton and Edwards, of America, and our own painstaking Kitto. The theory was also latterly and very ably advocated by the late Dr. Manson of Perth. On the other hand, for a *partial* deluge we have such distinguished men as Poole, Stillingfleet, Pye Smith, and Hugh Miller. The question is curious, but little for edification, and considering that the deluge was *miraculous*, it is futile to attempt to explain the miracle on natural principles or laws; and it will be found much less difficult to conceive of the waters extending over the whole circumference of the globe than covering a limited area. The fact of birds of the air being part of the consignment lends an argument to the universality of the flood. It is somewhat remarkable that the only two birds *named* are the raven and the dove, which are of the most common kind throughout the world. With reference to the second question many ingenious theories have been invented as to the mode of operation; but, as has been said, being a miracle, the ordinary laws of nature are superseded. The Christian will be content with the beautiful simplicity of the Scripture narrative. " The fountains of the great deep were broken up, and the windows (or rather the *floodgates*) of heaven were opened." The balance of the liquid element and the division made on the second great day or epoch of creation, when God "divided the waters which were under the firmament from the waters which were above the firmament," were thus disturbed. He once more, as at the dawn of creation, caused that the earth should " become void, and the Spirit of God moved upon the face of the waters."

A critical objection has been urged as to the adequacy of the ark to contain, together with food, for so long a period so great a variety of animals as are found throughout the world. We are very apt to form a too limited idea of the size of the ark and too great a conception of the number of its inmates. It must have been with some purpose that the exact proportions of the vessel are recorded. Dr. Hales, by a minute calculation, has proved that the ark was no less than 42,413 tons burden, which on calculation would carry 20,000 men. We are also apt to overrate the number of animals necessary to replenish the earth. The words of Scripture clearly distinguish between the genera or species—" fowls after *their kind*, and cattle *after their kind* and every creeping thing of the earth *after his kind.*" It is a well-known fact that animals, by change of climate and food, and especially by cross-breeding, eventually vary their character. Buffon even in his day calculated that 200 or 250 pairs of quadrupeds were sufficient for all the varieties of animal life falling under that class. Later discoveries have greatly limited this range. Sir Charles Lyell states, " It is a well-known and established fact that, through a variety of causes, from one original stock an almost endless variety has sprung up which are manifestly of *one species.*" On the authority of Darwin, " Naturalists are generally agreed that all the varieties of pigeons, and they are numerous and great, are descendants from the rock pigeon." Some Bible critics have perhaps unnecessarily argued for an additional creation of animals after the deluge. They rest their argument on the very peculiar words used in the covenant blessing, which was "with Noah and his seed after him, and with every living creature that is with him; from all that go out of the ark, *to every beast of the earth.*" This reading is further sought to be supported by a passage in Psalm civ., verses 29 and 30, which has an obvious reference to the deluge, and proceeds thus—" Thou hidest Thy face, they are troubled: Thou takest away their breath, they die, and return to their dust. *Thou sendest forth Thy Spirit, they are created: and Thou renewest the face of the earth.*" A curious and interesting fact may be mentioned as to the minute statement of the measurements of the ark. In the first place, it is remarkable how particular details are given as to dates during the whole history of the ark, especially as denoted by weeks or Sabbaths. This is the uniform test of *truth*. Falsehood delights in generalities to shun detection, but truth courts investigation by specialities. This renders probable what was formerly said, that the record may have been originally written by Noah himself, or Shem, who was with him in the ark. But the fact is, that the relative proportions of the diluvian vessel are now well ascertained to be the true proportions of a sound sailing vessel. It has been stated that Mr. Scott Russell, the eminent engineer, built the "Great Eastern" according to the precise rule laid down by divine direction to Noah. It is said that, like the antediluvians, many, whilst this leviathan ship was in progress of building, mocked and predicted that it would be found unmanageable when exposed to the tempest; it has, on the contrary, passed through fearful tempests without the least injury. No other vessel could be obtained of capacity to lay the various submarine cables which have united distant lands by the closest ties. Other vessels built on very different models, and deemed to be of vast strength, and constructed by greatest skill, have been found unfit for the strain of tempest, and in much less severe storms than what the Great Eastern has triumphantly passed scathless through, have successively been wrecked, and much national and individual loss been suffered.[1]

A difficulty has arisen, and been ably discussed, as to whether the rainbow had existence previous to the Deluge, or whether it was only then ap-

[1] It is, perhaps, not generally known that the eminent engineer now named is the son of a worthy Relief clergyman, recently deceased, who long ministered in the village of Errol in Perthshire.

pointed or set apart as a sign of the Covenant. It has been argued that the celestial phenomenon, being the result of natural laws existing previous to the Deluge, it could give no assurance that such a catastrophe should not again overwhelm the earth. By some learned men it has been supposed possible, nay probable, that there attended this great revolution of elements a change in the atmospheric canopy of the earth affecting the refrangible power of light in time of much rain. It has been proved that some of the planets of our system are altogether destitute of atmospheric girdles, and that others have more or less density and rareness of ether, and in this respect have varied between different periods of observation. Then as to the operation of light we have contending theories. The seeming paradox in the Mosaic record that light was created four days or periods of time before the sun, supposed to be its source and fountain, has been explained by the fact that the sun itself is a dark mass, and does not create, but only regulates, the fiery element with which it is surrounded, thus agreeing with the divine record as being set "to *rule* the day." The supposition of these philosophers gains support from several passages of holy writ. Thus, before the fall it is recorded that "the Lord God *had not caused it to rain* upon the earth, and there was not a man to till the ground. But there went *up a mist* from the earth, and watered the whole face of the earth." Again, *after* the fall, another change on the earth is indicated by the words, "Cursed is the ground for thy sake, in sorrow shalt thou eat of it all the days of thy life; thorns, also, and thistles shall it bring forth unto thee, and thou shalt eat the herb of the field." It is significant that our Redeemer was crowned at the crucifixion with thorns, as indicative of bearing the curse imposed on the ground for man's sake. Another change in natural law appears to have occurred at the Deluge. This is marked by the great diminution of the age of man, reduced at once from many hundreds to the term of 120 years. This may have had its cause in an atmospheric change detrimental to longevity, seeing that old age had been proved to have a tendency to sin and forgetfulness of the living God, in whom "we live, move, and have our being." Then there is a declared change of alimentary dietary law. It would appear that prior to the flood men were vegetarians, and that animals were only slain in sacrifice. After the flood it is announced that "Every moving thing that liveth shall be meat for you, even as the green *herb* have I given you *all* things." It cannot but be observed that whilst God has always made ample provision for human sustenance, there is ever some restriction, however small, to establish His sovereignty, and the free will and responsibility of man. Of *every* tree of the garden our first parents might *freely* eat, but of only *one* tree were they forbidden to eat, on the penalty of death. So, too, with the additional grant of animal food there was the one restriction, "But flesh with the life thereof, which is the blood thereof, shall ye not eat." Indeed, some divines have supposed and acted on the conviction that the same restriction is imposed under the New Testament. Some eminent Christians, both clerical and lay, have refused to partake of hare soup or fowls strangled. They found their objection on certain passages in the Acts of the Apostles. But on a close examination, these passages will be found connected with meats offered to idols, and with the obscene orgies generally practised at such pagan feasts.

It is not necessary to hold that the rainbow was created after the Deluge to mark that event, and give an assurance that it should no more return to devastate the earth. It is agreed by scholars that the words, "I do *set* my bow in the clouds," can, with equal propriety, be rendered "I do *ap-*

*point* or *set apart*" my bow in the cloud, to be a sign or token of the covenant between me and man. Numerous instances occur in Scripture of natural and even artificial objects being set apart as signs and memorials of events which had happened, and prophecies of what was to occur in the future. Let it be remembered that the fact remains that, whatever was the era of the creation of the celestial arch, it still proclaims hope and assurance that the earth never again will be consigned to a watery tomb, but that floods are temporary and local. So, too, it brings comfort and hope to the afflicted and sorrowing; and the darker the cloud and the denser the pitiless rain, the brighter shines the token of the Covenant.

> " Triumphal arch that fill'st the sky,
>     When storms prepare to part,
> I ask not proud philosophy
>     To teach me what thou art.
>
> For, faithful to its sacred page,
>     Heaven still rebuilds thy span,
> Nor lets the type grow pale with age
>     That first spake peace to man."
>                                         CAMPBELL.

The important subject of the Deluge cannot be well concluded without noticing that whilst its waters effectually swept the world from the possession of *sinners*, it was powerless, as was soon evidenced, to cleanse from *sin*. That required an element much more precious and potent—even the blood of God's own Son, whose name, by Heaven's decree, was *Jesus*, "because He should save His people from their *sins;*" not only from its consequences in penalty and punishment, but from its *power* and *dominion*. The existence of sin so soon after its merited judgment and punishment is significantly expressed in the words, "The wickedness of man was great in the earth, and *every imagination* of the *thoughts* of his *heart* was *only evil continually*," with the addition that this evil was "*from his youth.*" To escape from the *consequences*, rather than from *sin* itself, many have been, and are, the devices of man. Some in the pride of reason sought, and seek, to build intellectual towers, which they vainly imagine may "*reach unto heaven.*" Others, in their self-righteousness, have attempted, by their own efforts, to climb mountains more steep and high than Ararat. But all have failed, and all such efforts have proved abortive. The Ark of the Covenant, planned in the counsels of Omnipotence, with its one door (Jesus), and its one window (the Holy Spirit), alone affords a refuge for the sinner seeking to escape alike from the penalty and the power of indwelling sin. The invitation' is still as direct as in the days of Noah, "Come, thou and all thy house, into the ark." God is still as willing now as then to shut in those who have sought Jesus as the only remedy for sin and refuge for sinners. Let none imitate the antediluvian, and with the Ark of the new Covenant daily before his eyes, come too late and find the door shut against him.

> " Free was the offer, free to all, of life
> And of salvation, but the proud of heart,
> Because 'twas free, would not accept, and still
> To merit wished, and choosing, thus unshipped,
> Uncompassed, unprovisioned, and bestormed,
> To swim a sea of breadth immeasurable,
> They scorned the goodly bark, whose wings the breath
> Of God's eternal Spirit filled, for heaven,
> That stopped to take them in, and so were lost."

Two relics or symbols of the Deluge remain to this day, and are eminently fitted to add to the historical corroboration of the fact in the traditions of ancient nations. These reminiscences are the more interesting because emblematical of the deliverance of the saved and of the mercy of God. The divine record sets forth that the messenger of safety to the crew of the ark was a *Dove*, with its pledge of restored peace and love to the world after the war of waters. The *Olive Branch*, "newly plucked off," was not a stray vestige or waif of former destruction. Thus it is that we discover that in every age and land the dove has ever been and still is the emblem of *Love,* and an olive branch the emblem of *Peace.* There is nothing in the gentle animal or the humble plant which could recommend either of them to the nations of earth as such emblems, in preference to many birds of splendid plumage and melodious song, or to plants of finer mould, more gorgeous colour, or agreeable odour. The general reception of bird and plant as emblems and types of great principles and grand ideas can only have originated in some great event in which our common humanity had a deep and lasting interest. There is also an instructive truth in the name of the Dove. Its equivalent in ancient times was Jonah or Jonas, and in our own age John and Joanna. The prophet who carried the message of peace to Nineveh, about to be overwhelmed in destruction for iniquity (but how is untold), was appropriately Jonah, and a vegetable was the instrument to teach him that his God was a God of mercy. He, again, who was the messenger of glad tidings to a sinful and lost world, and the forerunner of Him who came to seek and save, had also the dove-like name of John, and that by express divine command, contrary to the desires and expectations of kindred, whose family record had no such familiar name. The Saviour of the world, on the presentation in the Temple, paid not the rich man's offering of the lamb of the first year, but came under the merciful provision for the poor, " If the mother be not able to bring a lamb, then she shall bring two turtle doves or two young pigeons." So, too, when the Holy Ghost descended on the Redeemer standing on the banks of Jordan, the Spirit was represented " like unto a dove." The dove was given by the Saviour to his disciples and to the Christian world as the emblem of all that is gentle, meek, and lovely in character. The beloved disciple who lay on the bosom of the Redeemer, and knew more than any of the apostles the mind of Jesus, whose epistles breathe love throughout, and whose last words are said to have been " Love one another," who before his departure was privileged to catch a glimpse of heaven and see the " Bow round about the throne " —his name was John. When Peter made the noble declaration of Christ's Messiahship, our Saviour immediately addressed him, not as Simon Peter or Cephas, but as " Simon Barjona, or *Son of the Dove.*" It is to be remarked that two of the four Evangelists —messengers of gospel or glad tidings, with beautiful feet on the mountains bringing glad tidings of great joy—are named John, for Mark, the second of the holy quaternion, was John, surnamed Mark. Seeing thus the remarkable Scriptural application of the name John as token of Love and Peace, it is strange that that name alone has been always thought unfortunate for Kings and Popes, so that when any who bear this gentle name assumed the crown or tiara, it was necessary that the name should be discarded, and one assumed thought to be more fortunate for such perilous distinctions. It may be mentioned as somewhat singular that the discoverer of America was named Columbus or the dove, and he who introduced Christianity into Scotland had the same dove-like name Columba, and that the seat of his residence was the isle of Iona, which might be read as John.

The other emblem or sign commemorative of the Deluge is the Bow or Rainbow. The divine record is brief but majestic in its brevity of this seal of the Noahic covenant—" I do set my bow in the cloud, and it shall be for a token of a covenant between me and the earth. And it shall come to pass when I bring a cloud over the earth, that the bow shall be seen in the cloud ; and the water shall no more become a flood to destroy all flesh. And the bow shall be in the cloud, and I will look upon it, that I may remember the everlasting covenant between God and every living creature of all flesh that is upon the earth." It is to be observed that this is the first time that the word covenant (bargain) occurs in Holy Writ. It is universally believed that the Bow mentioned in the record is the Rainbow. Nothing would be more likely to occur to the postdiluvians, especially when convinced of national sin, when rain fell in unusual quantities, than that divine justice was again to occasion to them a watery grave. This is especially thought to have been the object of the dwellers in Shinar, when they said one to the other, "Go to, let us build us a city and a tower, *whose top may reach unto heaven.*" Be this as it may, Josephus, the Jewish historian, observes that Noah was afraid, since God had determined to destroy mankind, lest he should drown the earth every year, but that God, in answer to his sacrifice and prayer, promised, "If I shall send at any time tempests of rain in an extraordinary manner, be not affrighted at the largeness of the showers, for the waters shall no more overspread the earth. But I will give you a sign that I have left off my anger by my bow." The promise of seed time and harvest as regular as day and night was an appropriate assurance of no general deluge, and in fact has been realized, since a partial famine in one part of the globe was always found to be coincident with a superabundance of cereal grain in another section of the earth's surface. It is seldom noticed how appropriate the sign of the Rainbow is to the promise of no general submersion of the earth in a watery gulf. The heavenly arch is never seen except when sudden and heavy rains fall on any special locality; then the beautiful span in heaven's canopy may assure the most timid heart that at no distant place there is a region where no rain descends and where the torrent is unfelt. The sun displays its great power by painting on the watery curtain its magic tints, with all the gorgeous beauty of creation's colouring—emblem of the Christian Church—"Unity in diversity, and diversity in unity."

> "When the waves that burst o'er a world accursed
>     Their work of wrath had sped;
> And the Ark's lone few, the tried and true,
>     Came forth among the dead.
> With the wondrous gleams of my braided beams
>     I bade their terrors cease,
> As I wrote on the roll of the storm's dark scroll
>     God's covenant of peace."

It is not surprising that the Rainbow has passed among all nations as the symbol of *Hope*. The proverbs of ancient nations testify to this. In China, *Tohi*, who is supposed to have been the founder of the celestial nation, is fabled to have been the son of a daughter of Heaven and conceived by her, being encircled by a Rainbow. The ancient Scandinavian mythology has the sublime idea that the Rainbow is the bridge which spans and connects earth with heaven. All classic poets revel in allusion to the Rainbow as a sign given by God to man, by heaven to earth. Homer writes—

> " Splendour diffusing as the various bow,
> Fixed by Saturnian Jove in showery clouds ;
> *A sign to mortal man.*" [1]

Virgil to the same effect—

> " These envied *rites* Saturnian Juno views,
> And sends the goddess of the various bow." [2]

So, too, the undoubtedly ancient but unquestionably apocryphal Book of Ecclesiasticus calls on man to " look upon the Rainbow, and bless Him that made it. It is very beautiful in its brightness. It encompasseth the heavens about with the circle of its glory, the hands of the Most High have displayed it" (Ecclesiasticus, xliii. 12, 13).

[1] " Ilias," xi., 27.   [2] "Æneidos," v., 605.

www.ingramcontent.com/pod-product-compliance
Lightning Source LLC
Chambersburg PA
CBHW031419160426
43196CB00008B/990